Zeuglodon

Alticamelus

Brontotherium

Ursus Spelaeus
(Cave Bear)

Teloceros

Woolly Rhinoceros

Uintatherium

Dinotherium

Woolly Mammoth

Imperial Mammoth

Prehistoric Animals

Prehistoric

Animals

Daniel Cohen

Illustrated by
Pamela Ford Johnson

Doubleday & Company, Inc.
Garden City, New York

For Charles Kent and
Jaimie Marie Hinckley

The editor wishes to thank Dr. John
Ostrom, professor of paleontology at
Yale University, for lending his
expertise in the preparation of this
book.

Book design by November and
Lawrence, Inc.
Art Direction by Diana Klemin
Library of Congress Cataloging-in-
Publication Data:
Cohen, Daniel.
    Prehistoric animals.

    Includes index.
    Summary: Discusses more than twenty
prehistoric animals, how they were
discovered, their modern counterparts,
and theories on their extinction.
    1. Mammals, Fossil—Juvenile
literature.   2. Birds, Fossil—Juvenile
literature.   3. Glacial epoch—Juvenile
literature.   [1. Prehistoric animals]
I. Johnson, Pamela Ford, ill.   II. Title.
QE881.C73   1988   569   86-19666
ISBN 0–385–23416–3
ISBN 0–385–23417–1 (lib. bdg.)

Something Terrible Happened

About 65 million years ago something terrible may have happened here on earth. The dinosaurs that had dominated the land for over 120 million years died off. The giant reptiles of the sea, such as the mosasaur (MO-zah-sawr), and the flying reptiles, such as the pterosaur (TAIR-ah-sawr), also disappeared. No one really knows why.

There are many theories. Some scientists believe that the climate changed and the dinosaurs couldn't adapt. Others think there may have been a great catastrophe. Perhaps the earth was struck by a giant meteorite; the dust from the impact would have blocked out the sunlight and cooled off the earth. Most paleontologists (pay-lee-on-TOL-oh-gists)—scientists who study ancient life—think a combination of events was involved. Whatever happened, life on earth at the end of the Age of Dinosaurs was suddenly very different than it had been before.

There were still plenty of animals alive, but those that remained were mostly small. Some reptiles, such as crocodiles and turtles, survived. On the land there were small insect-eating mammals. Small birds flew through the air. But the giants of land, sea, and air were gone.

Rise of the Mammals and Birds

Mammals evolved from reptiles. The first mammals appeared 200 to 220 million years ago. That's just about the same time that the first dinosaurs appeared.

Mammals are warm-blooded—that is, they maintain a constant body temperature, no matter what the outside temperature is. Their bodies are usually covered with hair. Most of them bear their young alive; they don't lay eggs. The young are nursed by their mother, not left to take care of themselves like the young of most reptiles.

The first birds appeared around 225 million years ago. Because they looked so much like small dinosaurs, scientists now believe that birds descended directly from dinosaurs. Like mammals, birds are warm-blooded. They have a body covering of feathers and most are adapted for flying. However, birds lay eggs.

As long as dinosaurs ruled the land, mammals could not compete with them. Most mammals were active at night when the giants slept. The birds too were a weaker group. They were unable to compete with the larger pterosaurs. With the giants out of the way, however, the small but active mammals and birds got their chance to take over the suddenly empty earth.

Triceratops

Insectivores

6

Ichthyornis

A New View of the Earth

People had been finding— and puzzling over—the bones of large unknown animals for centuries. Since they clearly were not the bones of known animals, people decided that they were the bones of dragons, unicorns, and other creatures of mythology and the imagination.

You might think that the gigantic bones people found belonged to dinosaurs. A few dinosaur bones did turn up, but such discoveries were rare. The dinosaurs died out so very long ago that their remains are hard to locate because they are usually buried deep in the earth. The bones that caused all the confusion were those of ancient elephants, rhinoceroses, gigantic bears, and other extinct mammals. These creatures had been dead for thousands—not millions—of years. Their remains were numerous, close to the surface, and well preserved.

About three hundred years ago scientists began to develop an entirely new view of the history of the earth. First they realized that the earth was much older than anyone had ever imagined. Later they discovered that the large and strange bones that had puzzled people for so long did not belong to dragons or unicorns but were the remains of extinct animals.

Some of these animals looked very much like living animals. The bones of the mammoth, for example, closely resembled the bones of modern elephants. Other animals were far stranger. Yet even the strangest generally bore some resemblance to living creatures.

These strange animals lived during the period scientists call the Cenozoic (SEE-nah-zo-ic), which means "recent animal life." The period is nearly 65 million years long, so it is recent only when compared to the 4.6-billion-year age of the earth itself. During the Cenozoic, also known as the Age of Mammals, the mammals thrived. But they weren't the only competitors for the world left by the dinosaurs.

Moa

The Real Big Bird

After the dinosaurs disappeared, the first animals to attempt to take over the land were birds. The fastest way for an animal to travel across flat land is to run. Some birds evolved that could not fly at all, but could only run. Soon a variety of large flightless birds developed. One of them, *Diatryma* (Die-ah-TRY-mah), was a giant. It was seven feet tall, with heavy bones and a huge beaked head. When it lived on the plains of what is now Wyoming, it was the biggest, fastest, and fiercest animal around.

Diatryma wasn't the only giant bird. In England, for example, there were flightless geese that were six feet tall. In South America there was a six-foot-tall flightless bird with a beaked skull the size of a horse's head. Some of these birds looked a lot like the two-legged dinosaurs. But the birds were not as successful as the dinosaurs. They had competition.

Mammals were also increasing in size and variety. While mammalian predators were no match for a full-grown *Diatryma,* they found the eggs of ground-living birds easy prey. By eating these eggs, the mammals were soon able to significantly reduce the number of large flightless birds.

Diatryma is long gone, but the ostrich, the emu, and the rhea still exist today. An even more gigantic bird, the moa, became extinct just a few hundred years ago. Moas were a group of heavy ostrich-like birds. The largest of them stood twelve feet tall. Great numbers of moas lived on the islands of New Zealand. They fell victim to the most dangerous of all mammalian predators—man. When the Maori people arrived in New Zealand, they soon hunted the moas to extinction.

Diatryma

Pouches and Egg Layers

A major difference between birds and mammals is that birds lay eggs and most mammals do not.

There are two main groups of mammals. By far the largest are the placental (plah-CEN-tal) mammals. They give birth to fairly well-developed young. Practically all of the mammals discussed in this book are placental mammals.

The marsupials (mar-SOO-pee-uls) also bear their young alive. But young marsupials are born in a very tiny and undeveloped state. They must spend time in their mother's pouch before they can go out on their own. The name "marsupial" comes from the Latin word meaning "pouch."

Marsupials were once much more common than they are today. Most marsupials now live in Australia. The kangaroo is the most famous of them—and the largest. The red kangaroo grows to a height of seven feet. Ten thousand years ago there was a ten-foot-tall kangaroo in Australia and a bear-like marsupial that was twelve feet long.

Duck-billed platypus

Opossum

Bear-like marsupial

Giant kangaroo

The most astonishing marsupial is the lowly opossum. It is the only marsupial that is common outside of Australia. There were opossums around at the time of the dinosaurs. Today, when many animals are being driven to extinction, this ancient creature gets along very well at the edge of the city. The opossum is one of the great success stories of mammal history.

Then there are the monotremes (MON-uh-treems), a tiny group of egg-laying mammals. The best-known is the duck-billed platypus of Australia. This strange-looking little creature has a body covered with fur, a bill and webbed feet like a duck, a broad flattened tail, and it lays eggs. Scientists once thought the platypus to be halfway between reptiles and mammals—the sort of animal from which all later mammals evolved. Now this theory is in doubt. No one knows quite what to think of this odd animal.

An Early Giant

One of the earliest of the giant mammals to evolve was also one of the strangest-looking. It is called *Uintatherium* (Yew-in-ta-THEE-ree-um) after the mountain range in Utah where its remains were first found. It was discovered at the same time that scientists were making spectacular dinosaur finds in the American West.

The beast had a headful of knobs and horns. Strangest of all were the enormous fangs that projected well over its lower jaw. When the bones of *Uintatherium* were first discovered, they created a lot of confusion. Scientists thought they might belong to a new kind of dinosaur. The fangs made them wonder if the beast was a carnivore. But further discoveries revealed that it was really a slow-moving, plant-eating mammal.

Uintatherium appeared about 60 million years ago, early in the Age of Mammals. The largest of these animals was twelve feet long and stood seven feet high at the shoulder. It was probably the largest land animal of its day.

For its size, *Uintatherium* had a tiny brain. Its threatening horns and thick hide were all the protection it needed from the smaller predators of the time. But this homely creature was unable to survive the changes in climate and the appearance of larger and more efficient predators.

Uintatherium

Brontotherium

The Thunder Beast

The Sioux Indians had stories of a gigantic animal they called the Thunder Beast. The legend may have begun when the Sioux found huge bones washed down from hillsides after a thunderstorm. Some of these bones were shown to the American paleontologist Othniel Charles Marsh. He recognized them as coming from an unknown type of ancient mammal. He named the creature *Brontotherium* (Bron-toe-THEE-ree-um), which means "thunder beast."

Brontotherium was a five-ton giant that was fifteen feet long and stood eight feet high at the shoulder. The animal's most spectacular feature was an enormous saddle-like horn on its nose. It was first believed that the horn was used as protection. But most of the predators that existed at the time *Brontotherium* lived were rather small. Its size was enough protection. It is more likely that the creatures used the horns in fights among themselves during the mating season.

Baluchitherium

The Largest Land Mammal

When Henry Fairfield Osborn of the American Museum of Natural History first looked at the hundreds of bone fragments that had been sent from Mongolia, he thought someone had made a mistake. "These pieces cannot all be from a single skull," he said. "Land mammals just don't grow this big."

No mistake had been made. All the fragments came from a single skull that was four and a half feet long. And the skull was small in comparison to the rest of the animal's body.

The first hint that such a creature existed came in 1911 when British scientists found partial remains of an enormous skeleton. They came from the part of the world we now call Pakistan. In 1911 it was called Baluchistan. The creature was named *Baluchitherium* (Ba-LUKE-eh-thee-ree-um). Much more complete remains, including the skull that so startled Osborn, were found in Mongolia in 1922.

Baluchitherium was a peaceful plant eater and the largest of all land mammals. It stood eighteen feet at the shoulder and with its long neck it could have nibbled at branches twenty-five feet high. If one of them were alive today, it could easily look into a second-story window. This giant weighed twenty tons, equal to the weight of five elephants. Though it didn't have a horn, *Baluchitherium* was most closely related to the rhinoceros.

"Foolish-footed"

Moropus (MORE-uh-pus) was a puzzle to scientists. The bones look like they come from two entirely different animals. The skull and body are quite horse-like. The animal was about the size of a modern horse. But the feet were very unusual. Instead of hooves, *Moropus* had large heavy claws. The feet looked as if they belonged to a giant anteater.

The bones of ancient animals are usually scattered. Sometimes the partial skeletons of several different animals are mixed together. For a long time that's what scientists believed had happened with *Moropus* skeletons. They thought they were finding parts of two different animals.

But then a complete skeleton was found. There could no longer be any doubt. The strange anteater's feet and the horse's body belonged together. That's why the creature was given the name *Moropus;* it means "foolish-footed."

Moropus was a plant eater. The claws which had so confused the scientists at first were probably used for digging up roots. The animal had very powerful shoulders and legs, so it must have been a strong digger. *Moropus* may also have used its big claws and powerful legs to drag down tree branches so that it could get to the leaves.

Moropus

Megaceros

Antlers and Horns

Deer and deer-like animals that evolved during the Age of Mammals sported impressive, sometimes spectacular antlers and horns. The most spectacular belonged to *Megaceros* (Mee-GAS-er-us), commonly called the Irish Elk.

Megaceros was a solidly built deer that stood about six feet high at the shoulder, making it the biggest known deer. But it was dwarfed by its own antlers. These could have been as huge as twelve feet across and four inches thick.

The tremendous antlers must have been useful for the male *Megaceros* in a fight for territory or for a female during the mating season. Otherwise they must have been a big problem. The antlers were so heavy that they could have overbalanced the animal when it leaned over to take a drink. The antlers may also have made it difficult for *Megaceros* to run away

from predators. This impressive creature died out a few thousand years ago, but many well-preserved remains have been found in Irish bogs.

Some of the early forms of deer, called protoceratids (pro-toe-SAIR-uh-tids), had horns on their noses as well as on the tops of their heads. Later deer, such as *Procranioceras* (Pro-cran-ee-oh-SAIR-uhs), had three antlers. Two stuck straight out and the third Y-shaped antler curved back over its neck.

Deer, even the giant *Megaceros*, shed their antlers and grew new ones every year. Other deer-like creatures—antilocaprids (an-till-oh-CAP-rids), for example—had true horns that were not shed. These horns were sometimes quite elaborate. *Ramoceros* (Ram-oh-SAIR-uhs) had short ruffled horns, while *Prolibytherium* (Pro-lib-ee-THEE-ree-um) looked like it was wearing a large bow tie on top of its head.

The Giant Ground Sloth

From 10 million years ago to a mere ten thousand years ago, one of the most common animals in South and later North America was *Megatherium* (Meg-uh-THEE-ree-um). It was a giant ground sloth. *Megatherium*'s closest living relatives are the tree sloths, which are small sleepy creatures that spend their lives hanging upside down from the branches of trees.

Megatherium, the largest of the giant ground sloths, was the size of an elephant. It spent most of its time sitting on its haunches and feeding on the leaves of trees, using its huge clawed front paws to pull branches within its reach.

When it moved, *Megatherium* walked on the sides of its feet with a clumsy shuffling gait. It couldn't run or even walk very quickly, but it didn't have to worry about being attacked. Its great size and powerful claws discouraged most predators. *Megatherium* also had a heavy coat of hair and its skin was studded with small bony plates. Biting into this well-protected creature would not have been easy, even for a large saber-toothed cat.

Megatherium

The "High Camel"

Alticamelus

You have probably seen a llama in the zoo. You may also have seen a giraffe there. Now try to imagine a llama as tall as a giraffe. You now have a pretty good idea of what *Alticamelus* (All-tee-ka-MEE-lus) looked like. The name means "high camel." These animals have also been called giraffe camels. They are the tallest known members of the camel family and among the tallest mammals of any kind ever found. The largest ones measured eighteen feet from the ground to the top of their heads. That's larger than most modern giraffes.

Alticamelus lived in the Western United States around 20 million years ago. The animal used its great size to eat the leaves from the tops of trees, just as the giraffe does today. No other plant eater could reach nearly as high, so *Alticamelus* didn't have much competition for food.

Camels first originated in Asia. They migrated to North and South America, where they flourished. Many different kinds of camels appeared during the Age of Mammals. However, around ten thousand years ago all of the camels in North America and many of the South American species died off. The llama, alpaca, and vicuña, small members of the camel family, still survive in South America.

The Armored Mammal

Glyptodon

Glyptodon (GLIP-toe-don) was the armored tank of the Age of Mammals. It wasn't quite tank-size, but at fourteen feet long and five feet tall, it was the size of a small automobile. Its back was covered by a rigid bony shell. At first glance, a *Glyptodon* skeleton bears a remarkable resemblance to the skeleton of a great turtle.

The creature's head was protected by a bony "helmet" and its tail was sheathed in bony rings. In some species the end of the tail had a spiked knob of bone that looked a lot like the club used by medieval knights. It probably served the same purpose. The animal could deliver a deadly blow to any attacker with its spiked tail. And if that wasn't enough, *Glyptodon* had huge claws on its front feet. The claws were usually used for digging up roots, but they made good weapons as well.

There were several species of *Glyptodon.* They lived mainly in South America, though remains of the creatures have also been found in the Southern and Southwestern parts of the United States. Their closest living relative is the armadillo.

Trilophodon

Dinotherium

Platybelodon

Moeritherium

An Explosion of Elephants

About 40 million years ago a pig-like creature called *Moeritherium* (More-eh-THEE-ree-um) lived alongside an ancient lake in Egypt. The creature was about three feet tall and had a longish nose. *Moeritherium*—or something very like it—was the ancestor of a large and varied tribe of elephants and elephant-like creatures.

Modern elephants are distinguished by three characteristics: great size, a long trunk, and huge teeth called tusks. Most ancient elephants also possessed these characteristics, but often with strange-looking variations.

Trilophodon (Try-LOF-oh-don) had a long lower jaw. In one type the lower jaw was an incredible seven feet in length! Tusks grew out of the end of the lower jaw and were apparently used for digging. The trunk extended only a little beyond the jaw and the curved upper tusks were used mainly for defense.

Dinotherium (Dine-oh-THEE-ree-um) didn't have any tusks in its upper jaw, but there were huge ones in its lower jaw. These curved downward. Scientists speculate that the tusks were used for uprooting plants.

Perhaps the most curious-looking relative of the elephant was *Platybelodon* (Plat-ee-BELL-oh-don). It has been nicknamed "shovel tusker" because its long lower jaw ended in two flattened tusks nearly four feet long. These creatures lived near the water and they used their lower jaw for "shoveling up" the enormous quantity of water plants they ate.

Mastodons and Mammoths

The best-known prehistoric relatives of the elephant are the mastodon (MAS-toe-don) and the mammoth (MAM-uth). Huge herds of these creatures roamed North America and the northern regions of Europe and Asia less than ten thousand years ago.

The American mastodon lived in the forests that covered much of North America after the retreat of the last glaciers. Large numbers of mastodon bones have been found in the Eastern United States. The American mastodon was not quite as large as today's elephants. Its tusks, however, were gigantic, as much as nine feet in length.

The mammoths are more closely related to modern elephants. There were several different species of mammoth. The largest, called the Imperial Mammoth, stood fifteen feet high at the shoulder. It was the largest elephant that ever lived.

More famous is the Woolly Mammoth. This was a creature of cold climates that lived at the edge of the glaciers. As the name indicates, it was covered with a thick coat of long hair. Though not the largest of elephants, the Woolly Mammoth did have the largest tusks. One of the great curving tusks measured as much as sixteen feet. The tusks curved outward and back toward one another. Sometimes they actually crossed. Since the points of the tusks were curved inward, they wouldn't have been much good in a fight. No one is quite sure how the Woolly Mammoth used its tusks.

The tusks of tens of thousands of mammoths have been found, mostly in Siberia. For many years the tusks of these ancient elephants were the world's main source of ivory. If someone you know owns an ivory object that was made a century or more ago, it might have been made from the tusk of a Woolly Mammoth.

American mastodon

Imperial mammoth

Frozen Mammoths

Our knowledge of prehistoric animals usually comes from finding their bones. But sometimes there is even more dramatic evidence.

From time to time the preserved remains of prehistoric animals—usually mammoths—have been found frozen in the ice in Alaska and particularly Siberia. The most well-preserved specimen was found in Siberia in 1806.

The animal had probably fallen off a cliff and died. Its body was then covered in a mud slide. The mud quickly froze and became part of the *permafrost*—that is, the part of the ground in very cold climates that never thaws. Many thousands of years later erosion wore away some of the frozen mud, exposing parts of the ancient elephant—to the astonishment of the local people, who thought it was some sort of underground monster.

There are stories that the mammoth had been quick-frozen in some sort of catastrophe and that when it was thawed the flesh was fresh enough to eat. That is an exaggeration. As parts of the creature began to thaw, the stench of decay was so powerful that no one wanted to go near it, much less eat any of it. It is true that the sled dogs would devour pieces of mammoth meat, but sled dogs are used to eating rotting meat.

This mammoth and other frozen mammoths show that the animals were covered with a thick coat of reddish hair. By examining the contents of their stomachs, scientists have even been able to find out what they were eating just before they died.

Woolly Mammoth

Teloceros

Woolly Rhinoceros

The Rhinoceros Family

Roaming the edge of the glaciers with the Woolly Mammoth was another large hairy beast—the Woolly Rhinoceros. In most ways the Woolly Rhinoceros looked like modern forms of the animal. The main difference is that it was covered by a thick coat of long hair. Today's rhinos are nearly hairless.

We know a lot about what the Woolly Rhinoceros looked like because of an unusual find in Poland. A completely preserved Woolly Rhinoceros was found in soil saturated with oil. The oil preserved the flesh and hair of the animal. Bones of the Woolly Rhinoceros have been found over a broad area of Europe, indicating that the creature was quite common for a long time.

The few species of rhinoceros that are alive today are rare and endangered. However, throughout the Age of Mammals there were many different types of rhinoceros. The name, incidentally, means "nose horn," though not all of them had horns on their noses.

The first rhinoceros appeared around 35 million years ago. It was about the size of a sheep and did not have a horn. *Baluchitherium,* the largest of all land mammals, was also a type of hornless rhinoceros.

A little over twenty million years ago a very peculiar-looking rhinoceros roamed North America. It was called *Teloceros* (TELL-oh-sair-us). It was a heavy clumsy looking creature with a little bump or knob at the end of its nose rather than a horn. Its legs seemed much too short for its heavy body. You might think such a creature would be a poor candidate for survival, yet it flourished for millions of years.

Saber-toothed Cats

The most fearsome predators among the prehistoric mammals were the saber-toothed cats, or stabbing cats. The most obvious feature of these cats were huge fangs. The saber-toothed cats are now all extinct. Modern cats are part of a group called the biting cats.

Largest of the saber-toothed cats was *Smilodon* (SMY-low-don). The name means "carving knife tooth" and it is appropriate, for the fangs were nine inches long. *Smilodon* was a little shorter than the modern lion, but much heavier and more powerfully built.

These great cats were not particularly fast, but they were well adapted to hunting and killing large prey. The neck was short and muscular. The fangs were used to stab and slash. The lower jaw could open so wide that it was completely out of the way during the animal's attack. The nose was pushed slightly back so that the cat could breathe while its face was buried deep in the thick fur of its victim.

The huge teeth present a problem. Scientists can't figure out how *Smilodon* and others of its kind were able to chew with such fangs. They speculate that the cats may have slashed big chunks out of their prey and swallowed them whole. Another theory is that the saber-toothed cats lived mainly on blood.

Some people have looked at the enormous fangs of the saber-toothed cats and decided that they became extinct because the fangs became too long. Scientists reject such an idea. They point out that a wide variety of saber-toothed cats had been very successful for some 35 million years. They died out less than ten thousand years ago.

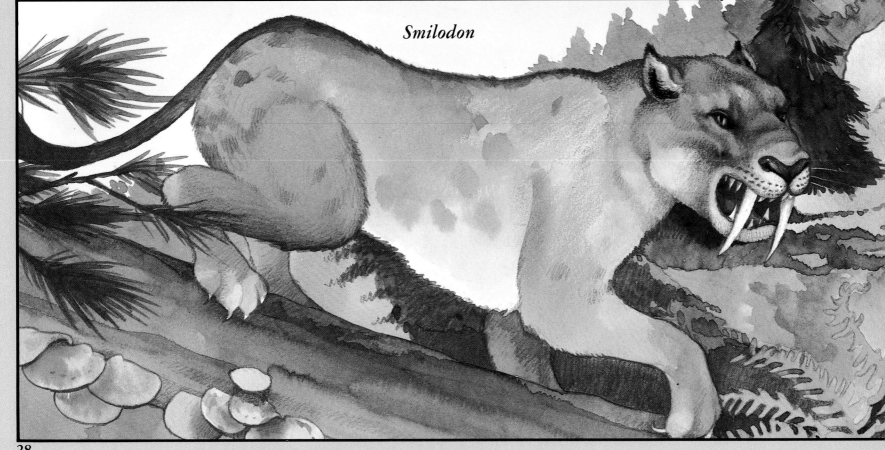

Smilodon

Felis atrox

Dire Wolf

Giant Jaguars and Wolves

The massively built saber-toothed cats preyed on large slow-moving plant eaters. They would even attack a young or injured mastodon or ground sloth. _Felis atrox_ (FEEL-is AY-trox), or "fierce cat," was built to run down swifter prey.

This animal was closely related to modern cats, particularly the jaguar, but it was much larger. Remains of these great predators have been found most often in caves or high rocky places. From such a vantage point _Felis atrox_ could have looked down upon the grazing herds below and picked its next victim with care.

The saber-toothed cats and _Felis_ _atrox_ were living in North America less than ten thousand years ago. At that time the most common predator was the Dire Wolf. A huge number of fossils have been found in the tar pits of Rancho La Brea, California. These deposits of sticky tar were a death trap for animals. The skeletons of Dire Wolves in the tar pits outnumber those of any other mammal. Packs of Dire Wolves must have attacked animals stuck in the tar and then become stuck themselves.

The Dire Wolf was like the modern wolf, except like most animals of the time it was larger and heavier than its modern counterpart.

Back to the Sea

Mammals are mainly land-living animals. One group of mammals, the bats, has adapted for flying. Another, the whales and porpoises, has adapted for a life in the sea. Flying imposes strict limits on size. The larger and heavier an animal is, the harder it is to get off the ground.

The sea imposes no handicap on size. In fact, great size can be a positive advantage and water will help support a creature's bulk. Therefore it is not surprising that the largest mammals, indeed the largest animals of any kind ever are seagoing mammals—the great whales—which are still alive today.

The fossil record for whales is spotty. Bones do not preserve well in the sea. Scientists believe that the distant ancestor of the whales was a cat-sized carnivore that lived by the seashore. It spent more and more time hunting in the water. Finally it became fully adapted to the sea.

One ancient whale that is well known is called *Zeuglodon* (ZOO-glow-don), and it lived 50 million years ago. *Zeuglodon* looked like the mythical sea serpent. The largest specimen grew more than seventy feet from the tip of its tooth-filled snout to the flukes on its tail. The front legs had evolved into powerful paddles, while the back legs disappeared entirely. The head was long and narrow, well adapted to catching and eating large fish. When *Zeuglodon* fossils were first discovered, people thought it was a sea serpent. Closer examination revealed it wasn't a reptile at all but a mammal.

Zeuglodon

The Cave Bear

Bears were the last carnivorous mammals to appear. The bear family dates back only 25 million years. The high point in the evolution of bears was reached during the Ice Age with *Ursus spelaeus* (UR-suss spee-LAY-us), the great Cave Bear.

As the name implies, these bears lived in caves throughout Europe. The Cave Bear stood about four to five feet high at the shoulder. When it stood up on its hind legs, as it often did, it could be ten feet tall.

In imaginary pictures of life during the Ice Age, the Cave Bear is often shown as a fierce fighter and a deadly enemy of the cavemen. In truth, the Cave Bear was mainly a vegetarian, though it had evolved from meat-eating ancestors.

Any animal as large and strong as the Cave Bear can be dangerous. But, like modern bears, the Cave Bear probably didn't seek out trouble and would attack only if attacked first.

The caves in which the remains of these bears have been found have provided a surprisingly good picture of the life of the Cave Bear. They were sociable, even playful creatures. In one cave the floor formed a stone chute that ended in a pool of water. Tracks leading to and from the chute indicate that the bears used it for sliding parties.

Ursus spelaeus

Cro-Magnon man

Neanderthal man

The Ice Ages

At the start of the epoch that scientists call the Pleistocene (PLIS-toe-seen), about 1.5 million years ago, the earth began to undergo dramatic changes. Great rivers of ice called glaciers began moving out of the north. They moved slowly, sometimes just a few feet every year, but they kept moving, flattening forests and gouging out valleys. The weather in the icy regions grew sharply colder. Eventually, much of North America, Europe, and Asia was covered with a thick sheet of ice. This was the Ice Age. It should more properly be called the Ice Ages, for the glaciers advanced and retreated several times. No one knows what caused the glaciers to expand—or to melt.

Many types of animals that were adapted to warmer weather moved southward, away from the advancing glaciers. Some died off because they couldn't adapt to the changing conditions. But many mammals adapted very well to the new colder world. The Woolly Mammoth and the Woolly Rhinoceros are examples of mammals that flourished during the Ice Age.

There was another type of mammal that also adapted very well to Ice Age conditions—man. There were two types of human being during the Ice Age. There was the fully modern type, our own direct ancestors, and a shorter, stockier type called Neanderthal (Nee-AN-der-thal) man. Despite his rather brutish appearance, Neanderthal man was fully human.

Both types of human being hunted the animals of the day. They sometimes made drawings of the animals they hunted on the walls of caves.

The Empty Land

This book started with the death of the dinosaurs 65 million years ago. You may have noticed that a lot of the animals described here died out about ten thousand years ago, at the end of the Pleistocene epoch. Although many large animals perished at that time, the extinction wasn't as drastic as the death of the dinosaurs. Plenty of large mammals survived, particularly in places like Africa and Southern Asia. But worldwide a high percentage of large mammals died out very suddenly.

The mass extinction was most severe in North America. Ten thousand years ago there were mammoths and mastodons, the giant sloth, and *Glyptodon.* Preying on the large plant eaters were the saber-toothed cats, *Felis atrox,* and the Dire Wolf. These are just a few of the large mammals that inhabited North America up to the end of the Pleistocene epoch.

A little less than five hundred years ago, when the first Europeans came to North America, the animal population was completely different. The moose and some large bears were around and millions of bison or buffalo roamed the plains. But the real giants were gone.

Scientists believe the big plant eaters died first. The large predators were left with nothing to hunt. They too soon became extinct.

What Happened to Them?

The reasons for the mass extinctions at the end of the Pleistocene have puzzled scientists for a long time. Many could not understand the sudden disappearance of so many different mammals.

One thing is sure: They didn't freeze to death in the Ice Age. The extinctions took place after the Ice Age had ended. In fact, many of these animals not only lived but prospered during the repeated advances and retreats of the glaciers.

When the Ice Age finally came to an end, the landscape had changed. The forests that had been home to the American mastodon were greatly reduced in size. But not all the habitats had changed. Let us look at the strange case of the horse.

Horses first evolved in North America. Then they spread all over the world. There were lots of horses in North America until the end of the Pleistocene epoch. Then, like so many other large animals, they disappeared. But horses did not die off in Asia. They were domesticated, taken to Europe, and ultimately brought back to North America by the Spanish.

Before the coming of the Spanish, the American Indians had never seen a horse. Some of the Spanish horses escaped to the Western plains. They found the land of their ancestors a very good place to live. Soon there were herds of wild horses in North America once again. If the land could still support wild horses, why did they die off in the first place?

Disease is a possible reason for extinction. For millions of years North America and Asia were connected. Animals migrated freely from one continent to another. During the Ice Age, the glaciers made migration much more difficult. Isolated from one another, the animals of Asia and the animals of North and South America became adapted to different diseases. When the ice melted and the animals of Asia and the Americas began to mix freely once again, they may have infected one another with new and deadly diseases.

Did Hunters Do It?

Some scientists now believe that human hunters were the main cause for the mass extinctions of large animals at the end of the Pleistocene epoch. Primitive man, armed with a spear, would be no match for a mammoth. A group of armed hunters might have been able to bring down one of the giants. But such a method of hunting would have been very slow and dangerous.

Around ten thousand years ago the human hunters discovered a new weapon—fire. Using torches or setting brush fires, a small group of human hunters could stampede a whole herd of mammoths over the side of a cliff. The animals might also be driven into a narrow canyon, where they could be killed with rocks and boulders.

It would have been an extremely wasteful form of hunting. No single tribe could use the meat from a herd of mammoths. But as far as the hunters were concerned, it was an easy way to get food and much safer than trying to kill a single large animal with a spear.

It is probable that hunting, disease, climate change, and other unknown factors contributed to the mass extinction of large mammals at the end of the Pleistocene epoch.

The Future

Prehistoric hunters didn't think about killing off large numbers of mammoths. They didn't worry about the future. They didn't think that one day there wouldn't be any more mammoths.

When hunters armed with rifles first went into the American West, they saw millions of bison. The hunters didn't worry about shooting them. But in less than a century the bison were nearly extinct.

Today hundreds of species of mammals, birds, and reptiles face extinction. They range from the little dusky sparrow to the great blue whale, the largest animal that has ever lived. Some animals are being hunted to extinction. Others face extinction because their habitats are being destroyed or poisoned by the by-products of civilization.

We can't be like the prehistoric hunters or the early bison hunters. We have to think about the future.

Fortunately, we have been. The bison was saved from extinction. Protection has assured the survival of the playful sea otter. A ban on DDT has helped to bring back our national symbol, the bald eagle, from the edge of extinction. Even in the poverty-stricken and overpopulated new nations of Africa, heroic efforts are being made to save endangered animals, such as the rhinoceros.

But the task of saving many of the world's strange and wonderful animals is far from over. What remains to be done is not easy. We are all going to have to cooperate.

Index

Africa   34, 39
Alaska   26
Alticamelus   20
American Indians   13, 37
Antilocaprids   17
Armadillo   21
Asia   20, 24, 33, 34, 37
Australia   10–11

Bald Eagle   39
Baluchitherium   15, 27
Bats   30
Bears   32, 34
Birds   5, 6, 8, 39
Bison   34, 39
Bones   7, 12–13, 15–16, 24, 26–27, 30
Brontotherium (Thunder Beast)   13

Camels   20
Caveman   32
Cenozoic period (Age of Mammals)
      7, 12, 27

Deer   17
Diatryma   8
Dinosaurs   5–7, 11, 34
Dinotherium   23
Dire wolf   29, 34
Dragons   7
Duck-billed platypus   11

Elephants   7, 23–24
Europe   24, 27, 32–33, 37

Fangs   28
Felis atrox   29, 34
Fire   38
Fossils   29–30

Giant ground sloth   18, 34
Giraffe   20
Glaciers   33
Glyptodon   21, 34

Horse   36–37
Hunters   38–39

Ice ages   32–33, 36–37

Jaguar   29

Kangaroo   10

Llama   20

Mammals
   body temperature   6
   extinction of   34, 36–37, 38–39
   future of   39
   marsupials   10–11
   monotremes   11
   placental   10
   rise of   6–7
Mammoths
   Imperial   24
   Woolly   24, 27, 33, 34, 38–39
Marsh, Othniel Charles   13
Mastodon   24, 29, 34, 36
Megaceros (Irish Elk)   17
Megatherium   18
Migration   37
Moa   8
Moeritherium   23
Mongolia   15
Moose   34
Moropus   16
Mosasaur   5

Neanderthal man   33
North America   12, 18, 20, 24, 27,
      33, 34, 36–37

Opossum   11
Osborn, Henry Fairfield   15

Pakistan   15
Paleontologists   5
Permafrost   26
Platybelodon (Shovel Tusker)   23
Pleistocene epoch   33–34, 36–38
Prolibytherium   17
Protoceratids   17
Pterosaur   5, 6

Ramoceros   17
Reptiles   5, 6, 39
Rhinoceros   7, 15, 27, 39
Rhinoceros, Woolly   27, 33

Saber-toothed cat   18, 28, 34
Sea otter   39
Sea serpent   30
Siberia   24, 26
Smilodon   28
South America   8, 18, 20–21

Tar pits   29
Teloceros   27
Tree sloth   18
Trilophodon   23
Tusks   23–24

Uintatherium   12
Unicorns   7
Ursus spelaeus (Cave Bear)   32

Whales   30

Zeuglodon   30

About the Author

Daniel Cohen is a well-known author of over one hundred books, many of them on science and related fields. Several of his works have been cited as outstanding books for children by various organizations, including the Children's Book Council, the National Science Teacher's Association, and the New York Public Library. He is also the author of *Dinosaurs,* another book you will enjoy.

Mr. Cohen resides in Port Jervis, New York, with his wife and daughter and five furry friends.

About the Artist

Pamela Ford Johnson is an award-winning illustrator whose lavish watercolors have appeared in over twenty children's books. Pamela is a graduate of the Paier School of Art in Hamden, Connecticut, where she also taught for ten years. In addition to painting, the artist enjoys carpentry and farming and keeps an aviary of Australian zebra finches. She lives in Connecticut with her husband, son, and daughter.

Felis Atrox

Smilodon

Dire Wolf

Trilophodon

Baluchitherium

Giant Kangaroo

Glyptodon

Moeritherium

Megaceros

Moropus

Platybelodon

Megatherium

Mastodon